Do You Want?

Written by Carol Ann Duffy
Illustrated by Alexandra Ball

Collins

Do you want a spy or a cook as a pal?

Or do you want a swimmer or a vet?

Can you have a pop star or a queen?

Do you want a juggler or a king as a chum?

Or do you want a painter or an elf?

Can you have a potter home for tea?

Do you want a singer or a boxer as a buddy?

Or do you want a farmer or a doctor?

Can you have a zoo-keeper at home?

Or what about a playmate just for you?

Do you want a frog or a snake as a pet?

Or do you want a zebra or a toad?

Can you keep a parrot on a perch?

Do you want a rat or a bat as a pet?

Or do you want a camel or a stork?

Will you keep a wolf on a porch?

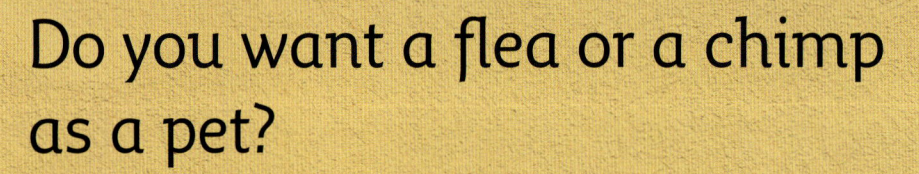

Do you want a flea or a chimp as a pet?

Or do you want a panda or a yak?

Will you have a fox in a shack?

Or what about a dog or a cat?

Do you want an igloo or a tent as a home?

Or do you want a cave or a nest?

Is a go-cart better than the rest?

Do you want a beach hut or a bus as a home?

Or do you want a kennel or a truck?

Will you pick a caravan as the best?

Do you want a ship or a van as a home?

Or do you want a tree top or a jet?

Will you pick a teapot as a home?

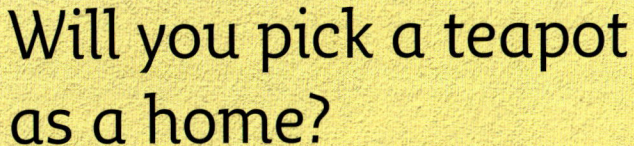

And stay in to play with a pal and a pet?

Do you want?

pal

14

pet

home

15

Ideas for reading

Written by Clare Dowdall, PhD
Lecturer and Primary Literacy Consultant

Reading objectives:
- demonstrate understanding when talking with others about what they have read
- read and understand simple sentences
- apply phonic knowledge and skills as the route to decode words
- learn to appreciate rhymes and poems

Communication and language objectives:
- express themselves effectively, showing awareness of listeners' needs
- listen to stories and respond to what they hear with relevant comments, questions or actions
- use spoken language to develop understanding through speculating and exploring ideas
- give well-structured descriptions, explanations and narratives

Curriculum links: Citizenship

Focus phonemes: a-e (snake), ea (beat), y (ee), y (spy), o-e (home)

Fast words: do, you, want, to, the, go, what, have

Resources: word cards of focus phonemes, whiteboard, pens

Word count: 276

Build a context for reading

- Revise the focus phonemes using word cards.
- Ask children: *If you could have anything in the world, who would you like as a friend, where would you like to live, and what would you like for a pet?*
- Look at the front cover and read the title together. Help them to read the fast word *want* and ensure they understand how to sound out the *a* phoneme in this word. Explain that this is a poem about making choices. Look at the front cover illustration and as a group discuss what they think the child in the picture has chosen.

Understand and apply reading strategies

- Turn to pp2-3. Model reading the questions on these pages, emphasising the repeating questioning pattern. Note how the poem's lines are structured, and check they can decode the word *spy* and that they know what it means.
- Ask children to respond to the poem by choosing from each pair of ideas on pp2-3 and sharing and justifying their choices with the group.